KANSAS CITY CHIEFS

BY JOSH ANDERSON

Stride
An Imprint of The Child's World®
childsworld.com

The Child's World
childsworld.com

Published by The Child's World®
800-599-READ • www.childsworld.com

Photography Credits
Cover: © Jamie Squire / Staff / Getty Images; page 1: © Africa Studio / Shutterstock; page 3: © Cliff Hawkins / Staff / Getty Images; page 5: © Jamie Squire / Staff / Getty Images; page 6: © AP / Associated Press; page 9: © Kevin C. Cox / Staff / Getty Images; page 10: © Jason Hanna / Stringer / Getty Images; page 11: © stevezmina1 / Getty Images; page 12: © Jamie Squire / Staff / Getty Images; page 12: © Christian Petersen / Staff / Getty Images; page 13: © JERILEE BENNETT/KRT / Newscom; page 13: © Jamie Squire / Staff / Getty Images; page 14: © Peter Aiken / Stringer / Getty Images; page 15: © Kyle Rivas / Stringer / Getty Images; page 16: © Amineshaker / Wikimedia; page 16: © Jeff Gross / Staff / Getty Images; page 17: © Brian Bahr / Staff / Getty Images; page 17: © Tim DeFrisco / Stringer / Getty Images; page 18: © File Photo/MCT / Newscom; page 18: © Tony Tomsic / SportsChrome / Newscom; page 19: © Justin Edmonds / Stringer / Getty Images; page 19: © Jamie Squire / Staff / Getty Images; page 20: © Kevin C. Cox / Staff / Getty Images; page 20: © Mike Ehrmann / Staff / Getty Images; page 21: © Stacy Revere / Stringer / Getty Images; page 21: © Bob Levey / Stringer / Getty Images; page 22: © Robert B. Stanton / Stringer / Getty Images; page 23: © Jonathan Daniel / Stringer / Getty Images; page 23: © stevezmina1 / Getty Images; page 25: © Jamie Squire / Staff / Getty Images; page 26: © Frederick Breedon / Stringer / Getty Images; page 29: © Jason Hanna / Stringer / Getty Images

ISBN Information
9781503857803 (Reinforced Library Binding)
9781503860537 (Portable Document Format)
9781503861893 (Online Multi-user eBook)
9781503863255 (Electronic Publication)

LCCN 2021952630

Printed in the United States of America

BRINGING THE WORLD 19 68 TO YOUNG READERS

TABLE OF CONTENTS

GO CHIEFS!

The Kansas City Chiefs compete in the National Football **League's** (NFL's) American Football Conference (AFC). They play in the AFC West **division**, along with the Denver Broncos, Las Vegas Raiders, and Los Angeles Chargers. Fans in Kansas City have been lucky! Their Chiefs made the **playoffs** every season between 2015 and 2021. The Chiefs won the **Super Bowl** in 2019 and made it back to the big game in 2020. Let's learn more about the Chiefs!

AFC WEST DIVISION

Denver Broncos

Kansas City Chiefs

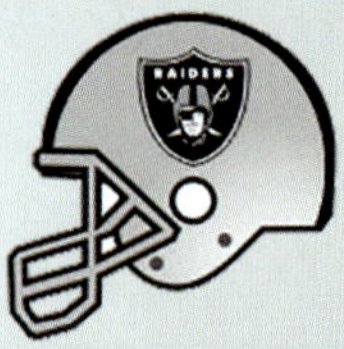

Las Vegas Raiders

Los Angeles Chargers

THE CHIEFS WON THE AFC WEST DIVISION TITLE FOR SIX STRAIGHT SEASONS FROM 2016 TO 2021.

BECOMING THE CHIEFS

The team was formed and originally played in Dallas, Texas. They were called the Dallas Texans when the team began play in 1960. They were part of the American Football League (AFL). In 1963, the team moved to Kansas City, Missouri, and became the Chiefs. The Chiefs joined the NFL when the AFL and NFL combined in 1970. The Chiefs played in the first-ever Super Bowl after the 1966 season. They lost to the Green Bay Packers 35–10.

QUARTERBACK LEN DAWSON (LEFT) PLAYED FOR THE CHIEFS FOR MORE THAN A DECADE.

BY THE NUMBERS

The Chiefs have won **TWO** Super Bowls.

16
division titles for the Chiefs

565
points scored by the team in 2018—a Chiefs record!

14
wins for the Chiefs in 2020

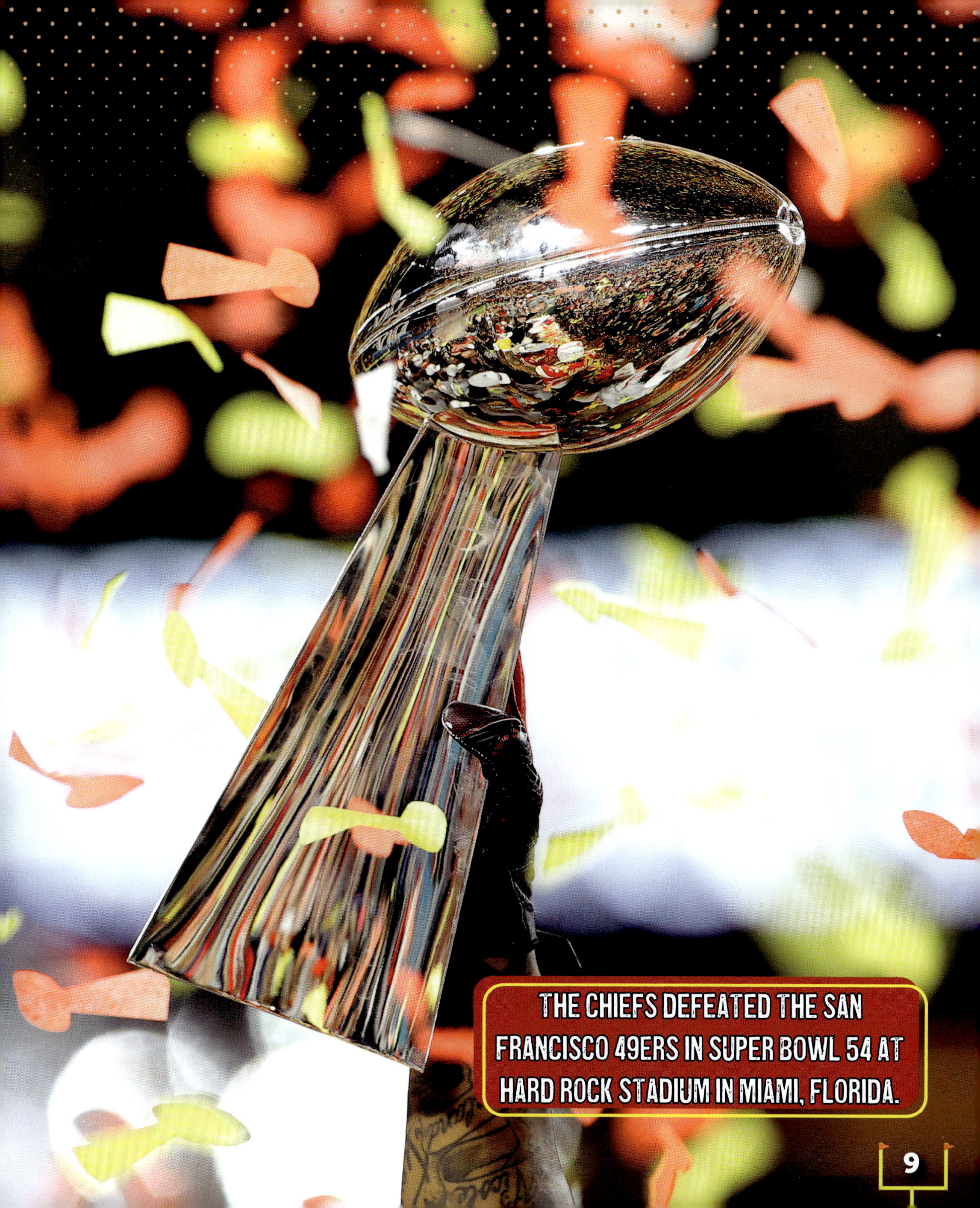

THE CHIEFS DEFEATED THE SAN FRANCISCO 49ERS IN SUPER BOWL 54 AT HARD ROCK STADIUM IN MIAMI, FLORIDA.

CHIEFS FANS ARE SO DEDICATED TO THEIR TEAM THAT A WINTER STORM DID NOT STOP THEM FROM FILLING ARROWHEAD STADIUM FOR A PLAYOFF GAME IN 2019.

GAME DAY

The Chiefs play their home games at GEHA Field at Arrowhead **Stadium**. In their early days, the team shared Municipal Stadium with the Kansas City Athletics and the Kansas City Royals Major League Baseball teams. Arrowhead Stadium has been the team's home since 1972. The building holds up to around 76,000 Chiefs fans. During one game in 2014, the crowd at Arrowhead was so loud, it set a Guinness World Record! The crowd hit 142.2 decibels! That's louder than a normal police siren!

We're Famous!

The video game *Madden NFL* features one or more players on the game's cover each year. But until recently, no player ever appeared on the cover more than once. That changed with the release of *Madden NFL 2022*. Tampa Bay Buccaneers quarterback Tom Brady and Chiefs quarterback Patrick Mahomes became the game's first-ever repeat cover athletes!

UNIFORM

RED

WHITE

Truly Weird

During one game in 1990, Broncos quarterback John Elway was so bothered by the crowd noise at Arrowhead Stadium that he asked the referee for help! The ref got on the microphone and threatened to charge the Chiefs with a timeout if the crowd didn't quiet down. Some in attendance believe the fans got louder after that! The ref didn't follow through on his threat, and the Chiefs won the game 31–20.

Alternate Jersey

Sometimes teams wear an alternate jersey that is different from their home and away jerseys. It might be a bright color or have a unique theme. To celebrate the AFL's 50th anniversary in 2009, the Chiefs wore "throwback" Dallas Texans uniforms for two games that season.

SPECIAL EFFECTS MAKE PLAYER INTRODUCTIONS AT ARROWHEAD STADIUM MORE EXCITING FOR THE FANS BEFORE GAME TIME.

TEAM SPIRIT

Going to a game at Arrowhead Stadium can be a ton of fun! Chiefs fans often replace the final words of the national anthem ("home of the brave") with "home of the Chiefs." The Chiefs Cheerleaders entertain the crowd during breaks in the action. The team's mascot is KC Wolf, a giant costumed gray wolf. Fans looking for some high culture before or after the game can enjoy the stadium's Arrowhead Art Collection. And visitors looking for a unique snack can try a waffle sandwich with cheese, jam, lettuce, tomatoes, and more at Peace, Love & Waffles.

KC WOLF

HEROES OF HISTORY

Len Dawson

Quarterback | 1962–1975

Dawson led the Chiefs to their first Super Bowl victory after the 1969 season. He's the **franchise** leader with 28,507 passing yards and 237 **touchdowns**. Dawson was chosen for the **Pro Bowl** seven times and is a member of the Pro Football **Hall of Fame**.

Priest Holmes

Running Back | 2001–2007

Holmes scored 83 total touchdowns in 65 games with the Chiefs. His 27 rushing touchdowns in 2003 ranks second all-time for a single season. Holmes rushed for more than 4,500 yards from 2001to 2003. He was chosen for the Pro Bowl in all three of those seasons.

Will Shields

Guard | 1993–2006

Shields started every game of his entire 14-year career except the first. The 12-time Pro Bowler also never missed a game due to injury. Shields helped lead the team to the playoffs six times. He was inducted into the Pro Football Hall of Fame in 2015.

Derrick Thomas

Linebacker | 1989–1999

Thomas is the Chiefs' all-time leader in **sacks** with 126.5. In one contest in 1990, he set the single-game record with seven sacks. Thomas was chosen for the Pro Bowl nine times. He is a member of the Pro Football Hall of Fame.

The Chiefs represent the AFL in the first-ever Super Bowl. The NFL's Green Bay Packers win 35–10.

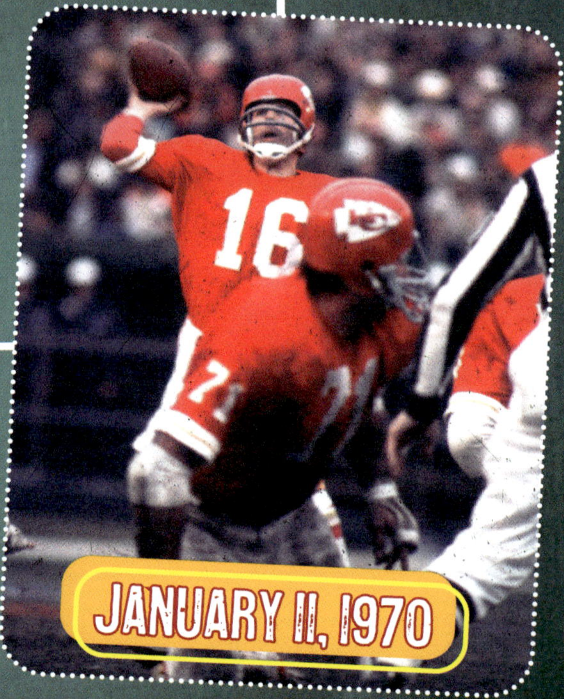

The Chiefs make it back to the Super Bowl. This time they win, defeating the Minnesota Vikings 23–7.

BIG DAYS

APRIL 27, 2017

The Chiefs select Patrick Mahomes with the tenth pick in the first round. Mahomes quickly becomes one of the NFL's top passers.

JANUARY 24, 2021

The Chiefs play the Buffalo Bills in the AFC Championship Game. Kansas City wins 38–24 and earns their second straight trip to the Super Bowl.

MODERN-DAY MARVELS

Travis Kelce

Tight End | Debut: 2013

In 2020, Kelce passed Otis Taylor's 7,306 receiving yards and became the second-leading receiver in franchise history. Kelce had over 1,000 yards receiving every season from 2016 to 2021. He earned trips to the Pro Bowl each year from 2015 to 2021.

Patrick Mahomes

Quarterback | Debut: 2017

Mahomes won the NFL's **Most Valuable Player** Award during his first year as a starting quarterback in 2018. That year, he passed for 50 touchdowns, the second most ever in a single season. He led the Chiefs to a Super Bowl victory in 2019 and back to the big game in 2020.

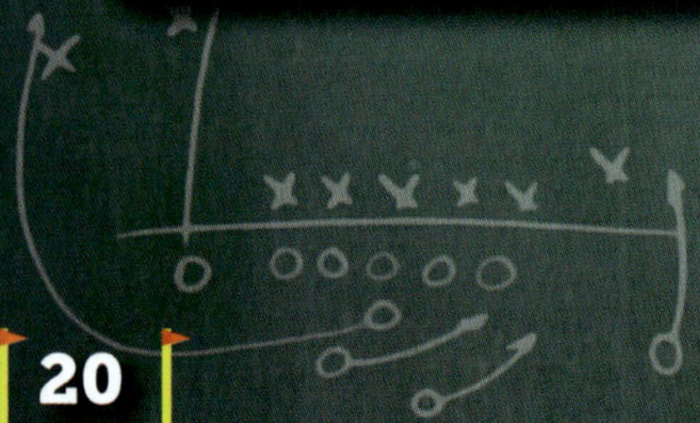

Tyrann Mathieu

Safety | Debut: 2019

Mathieu helped lead the Chiefs to the Super Bowl during his first two seasons with the team. He led all safeties with six interceptions in 2020. Standing only 5 feet, 9 inches (175 cm) tall, Mathieu earned the nickname "Honey Badger" for his willingness to compete with much larger opponents.

Justin Reid

Safety | Debut: 2022

Reid played his first four seasons for the Houston Texans. He signed with the Chiefs before the 2022 season. Reid started 53 of the 57 games he played for the Texans. He finished with more than 75 combined tackles in his first three seasons. He's shown here in his old Texans uniform.

TONY GONZALEZ PLAYED 12 SEASONS OF HIS CAREER WITH THE CHIEFS.

THE GOAT

GREATEST OF ALL TIME

TONY GONZALEZ

Gonzalez played 12 seasons for the Chiefs. He ranks first among tight ends, and sixth overall, in NFL history with 15,127 receiving yards. His 10,940 yards and 76 touchdown catches as a Chief are the most in franchise history. In 2004, Gonzalez led the league with 102 catches. He was selected for the Pro Bowl in 14 of his 17 seasons. Gonzalez was inducted into the Pro Football Hall of Fame in 2019.

#1

FAN FAVORITE

Christian Okoye–Running Back

1987–1992

Okoye was beloved by fans for his powerful running and tackle-breaking ability. Okoye was born in Nigeria, a country in Africa. Fans called him the "Nigerian Nightmare." He led the NFL in rushing in 1989 when he gained 1,480 yards.

THE BIG GAME

FEBRUARY 2, 2020 – SUPER BOWL 54

The Chiefs earned a trip to the Super Bowl after the 2019 season for the first time in 50 years. Their opponent in the big game was the San Francisco 49ers. The 49ers had one of the best defenses in the league. The Chiefs trailed 20–10 with just over six minutes left in the game. Patrick Mahomes threw a touchdown pass to Travis Kelce to cut the 49ers' lead to 20–17. With under three minutes to play, the Chiefs took the lead 24–20 on another Mahomes touchdown pass. In the end, they won the game 31–20.

PATRICK MAHOMES THREW FOR 286 YARDS WITH TWO TOUCHDOWN PASSES IN SUPER BOWL 54.

ANDY REID HAS COACHED THE CHIEFS IN 13 POSTSEASON GAMES.

AMAZING FEATS

5,097
Passing Yards

In 2018 by
QUARTERBACK
Patrick Mahomes

1,789
Rushing Yards

In 2006 by
RUNNING BACK
Larry Johnson

15
Touchdown Receptions

In 2010 by
WIDE RECEIVER
Dwayne Bowe

22
Single-Season Sacks

In 2014 by
LINEBACKER
Justin Houston

ALL-TIME BEST

PASSING YARDS

Len Dawson
28,507

Trent Green
21,459

Patrick Mahomes
18,991*

RUSHING YARDS

Jamaal Charles
7,260

Priest Holmes
6,070

Larry Johnson
6,015

RECEIVING YARDS

Tony Gonzalez
10,940

Travis Kelce
9,006*

Otis Taylor
7,306

SACKS**

Derrick Thomas
126.5

Tamba Hali
89.5

Neil Smith
85.5

SCORING

Nick Lowery
1,466

Jan Stenerud
1,231

Harrison Butker
671*

INTERCEPTIONS

Emmitt Thomas
58

Johnny Robinson
57

Deron Cherry
50

*As of 2021
**unofficial before 1982

RUNNING BACK JAMAAL CHARLES LED THE NFL WITH 12 RUSHING TOUCHDOWNS IN 2013.

GLOSSARY

division (dih-VIZSH-un): a group of teams within the NFL who play each other more frequently and compete for the best record

franchise (FRAN-chyze): a professional sports team

Hall of Fame (HAHL of FAYM): a museum in Canton, Ohio, that honors the best players in NFL history

league (LEEG): an organization of sports teams that compete against each other

Most Valuable Player (MOHST VAL-yuh-bul PLAY-uhr): a yearly award given to the top player in the NFL

playoffs (PLAY-ahfs): a series of games played after the regular season that decides which two teams play in the Super Bowl

Pro Bowl (PRO BOWL): the NFL's All-Star game where the best players in the league compete

sack (SAK): when a quarterback is tackled behind the line of scrimmage before he can throw the ball

stadium (STAY-dee-uhm): a building with a field and seats for fans where teams play

Super Bowl (SOO-puhr BOWL): the championship game of the NFL, played between the winners of the AFC and the NFC

touchdown (TUTCH-down): a play in which the ball is brought into the other team's end zone, resulting in six points

FIND OUT MORE

IN THE LIBRARY

Bulgar, Beth and Mark Bechtel. *My First Book of Football.* New York, NY: Time Inc. Books, 2015.

Jacobs, Greg. *The Everything Kids' Football Book, 7th Edition*. Avon, MA: Adams Media, 2021.

Sports Illustrated Kids. *The Greatest Football Teams of All Time*. New York, NY: Time Inc. Books, 2018.

Wyler, Zach. *Kansas City Chiefs*. New York, NY: AV2 Books, 2022.

ON THE WEB

Visit our website for links about the Kansas City Chiefs:
childsworld.com/links

Note to parents, teachers, and librarians: We routinely verify our web links to make sure they are safe and active sites. Encourage your readers to check them out!

INDEX

ABOUT THE AUTHOR

Josh Anderson has published over 50 books for children and young adults. His two boys are the greatest joys in his life. Hobbies include coaching his sons in youth basketball, no-holds-barred games of Apples to Apples, and taking long family walks. His favorite NFL team is a secret he'll never share!